AMBROSIA
HAWTHORN

Zodiac Magic

Astrological Wisdom for
Love, Work and Family

Illustrations by
Silvia Vanni

ixia
PRESS

Garden City, New York

Contents

Zodiac Magic

Publisher: Balthazar Pagani
Edited by Vittoria Mieli
Drafting: PEPE *nymi*
Graphic Design: Eleonora Tallarico / PEPE *nymi*

Translation: TperTradurre s.r.l., Rome
Editing: Andrea Modica

Vivida

Vivida® is a registered trademark property of White Star s.r.l.
www.vividabooks.com

Copyright

Bibliographical Note

This Ixia Press edition, first published in 2024, is a modified
English translation of *Zodiac Magic: Understand to Influence*,
originally published in Italian by Vivida, an imprint of
White Star Publishers, Milan, in 2023.

International Standard Book Number

ISBN-13: 978-0-486-85175-4
ISBN-10: 0-486-85175-3

IXIA PRESS
An imprint of Dover Publications

Manufactured in Italy
85175301   2023
www.doverpublications.com/ixiapress

Fire signs

Aries
31

Leo
45

Sagittarius
59

Earth signs

Taurus
75

Virgo
89

Capricorn
103

Air signs

Gemini
119

Libra
133

Aquarius
147

Water signs

Cancer
163

Scorpio
177

Pisces
191

○———————○

Welcome, I am so happy you are here! My name is Ambrosia. I am an independent witch and the founder of *Witchology*, a magazine for contemporary witches. A large part of my practice contains "cosmic witchcraft": I integrate my magical knowledge with the wonderful and surprising world of astrology. Any kind of magic can be enhanced by the astrological correspondences! A famous saying amongst us witches goes **"as above, so below"**: the movements of the stars and celestial energies influence events on Earth. We can see them through the tides and in the changing of the seasons, and also by merely observing the different aspects of our personalities based on the planets that govern us and make up our astral plane. I wish to share my knowledge with you because, as you will see, astrology is a powerful tool in making the most of the energy that reverberates throughout the universe and echoes in everything that surrounds us: people, animals, plants, and objects.

Each sign of the zodiac is ruled by one or more planets; their influence determines the characteristics that make you unique and unrepeatable. This book will take us on a journey to discover the basic principles of astrology founded on the twelve signs of the zodiac.

○———————○

I offer you the gift of the tools to create a personal relationship with the energy associated with each celestial body. I will teach you how to create simple magical potions connected to the specifics of each sign, the phases of the moon, and the seasons. I will show you how to create little amulets to kindly protect the people you most care about and to strengthen your luck in love, with your family, and at work. I will reveal some simple readings from the Major Arcana of the tarot to help you bring clarity to your heart. For each sign you will find the relationship between your astral plane and the planets within it, your compatibility with the other signs, and a brief guide to teach you about the astrological significance of the elements, the planets, and the astral houses.

Let's go together on a discovery of your very own place in the stars.

Remember, every journey can be magical. It all depends on you.

Ambrosia Hawthorn

(By the way, I am a Taurus Sun
and a Libra Moon, and I have
a Sagittarius Ascendant.)

Introduction

✦ Your Birth Chart ✦

Your birth or star chart is a map showing the transition of the planets and the aspects that formed between them at the exact time of your birth, revealing precious insight into your personality, how you love, what you desire, and your goals.

Graphically, it is a circular wheel divided into twelve sections, or houses, each coinciding with a sign of the zodiac. Each section marks the planets that were transiting in the sky at the moment of your birth. For example, a Leo may have Mars in Libra.

Your birth chart is calculated using the location, date, and time of your birth. The more the details are exact, the more accurate your chart will be. In order to get the most out of this book, it is necessary to have your birth chart handy.

The simplest and quickest way to calculate your birth chart is through one of the tools you can find on the many specialized Internet sites; just type "calculate birth chart" into your search engine.

Before we begin exploring the various aspects of your birth chart, let me briefly explain the meaning and characteristics of the various houses and planets.

✦ The Houses ✦

The houses are the twelve areas of your birth chart that represent important parts of your life, such as identity, love, money, career, family, purpose, and health, to name a few.

Houses that relate to romantic compatibility: **5th, 7th, 8th**
Houses that relate to family compatibility: **4th, 5th, 7th, 10th**
Houses that relate to work compatibility: **2nd, 3rd, 7th, 9th, 10th**

House Name Meaning

HOUSE	NAME	MEANING
1st	**House of Self**	Physical self, self-image, identity, personality, outlook on life, ego
2nd	**House of Values**	Material possessions, money, security, self-worth, self-esteem
3rd	**House of Communication**	Thoughts, verbal and written communication, learning style, skills, talents, technology, knowledge, transportation, travel, relationships with neighbors and siblings
4th	**House of the Family**	Inner life, ancestry, heritage, home affairs, environment, relationships with parental figures, housing, upbringing, neighborhood, comfort, security, pets
5th	**House of Creativity**	Self-expression, joy, leisure activities, entertainment, playing, games, romance, creativity, children
6th	**House of Work**	Daily routines, skills, diet, duties, work, strength, mentoring, wellness, courage, health

7th	House of Relationships	Partnerships, marriage, cooperation, diplomacy, agreements, contracts, collaboration, relationships of all kinds
8th	House of Transformation	Intimacy, psyche, spirituality, cycles, change, death, sexual relationships, commitments, self-transformation, shared resources, karma, debt, joint finances
9th	House of Journeys	Higher self, wisdom, higher learning, illumination, journeys, philosophy, foreign affairs, culture, expansion, ethics, belief systems, exploration
10th	House of Ambition	Motivation, public self, reputation, mission, career, visibility, power, ambition, career achievements, society, government, authority, status, parental relationships
11th	House of Friendship	Community, friends, creative groups, expression, social, like-minded people, new ideas, effort, belonging, charity, networking, wishes
12th	House of Secrets	Privacy, refuge, emotional responses, dreams, meditation, seclusion, intuition, addiction, luck, healing, cleansing, completion, conclusion, forgiveness, peace

✦ 1st House ✦

The first house is the House of Self and defines you, your sense of awareness, and your self-image. It's home to the Ascendant, or Rising, sign. If you are born with other planets in this house, they are important to your identity. If there are no other planets in this house, that means this isn't an area that needs your attention. The more planets that are clustered together in one house, the more attention you might need to pay it. Different houses or areas in your life will require a different degree of attention. For more on your identity and purpose, look to see where the Sun is located in your chart.

✦ 2nd House ✦

The second house is the House of Values. It highlights your relationship with the material world, money, and security. You'll find important insights into your self-worth, self-esteem, and ability to make and spend money. Planets located within this house will help you understand what level of security you're after and what is important to you in your career. For more insight into what you value in life, look at where Venus is located in your chart.

✦ 3rd House ✦

The third house is the House of Communication, and it shows how you communicate, think, and learn. This house is important for learning more about your communication style and how you connect with your partners, family, and coworkers. An empty third house means that you're a comfortable communicator, but one or more planets reveal their importance to you in your life. Make sure to check which sign Mercury is in on your birth chart to learn more about the other half of how you communicate.

✦ 4th House ✦

The fourth house is the House of the Family; it shows how you relate to your birth family, your hometown, and your roots, as well as your need for security and the bases on which you wish to build something important. In the wider sense, it also represents your relationship with material goods and property. It is an important house, as it represents one of your intimate and authentic sides rather than your public image, which is represented by the tenth house. For more accurate information on how you relate with familiar effects, check the location of the Moon in your birth chart.

✦ 5th House ✦

The fifth house is the House of Creativity. It indicates your creative abilities in a moral and material sense and represents the way in which you affirm your identity: how you spend your free time, how much space you allow for enjoying yourself and playtime, what your artistic gifts are. It also outlines your idea of parenthood, as procreation is intended as a creative act. Check the Sun's location in your birth chart if you want more accurate information on this aspect.

✦ 6th House ✦

The sixth house is the House of Work. It rules the kingdom of duties and everyday responsibilities and indicates how you take care of your concrete needs and look after others. It also explains your relationship with your body and your health—if there are no planets in this house, you can probably take for granted that your body is functioning well and that your immune system works. For more information on this theme, take a look at Mercury's location in your birth chart.

✦ 7th House ✦

The seventh house is the House of Relationships and what is "other than yourself." It indicates the way in which you enter sentimental relationships and with what spirit and intensity you share intimacy with others. Based on the planets present in this house in your birth chart, you will find information on the nature of your personal relationships. As it is found opposite the first house, which represents your Ascendant sign, the seventh house represents your Descendant sign. Check the location of Venus in your birth chart for further information on these aspects.

✦ 8th House ✦

The eighth house is the House of Transformation. It indicates the resources you use to get through crises and traumatic moments in order to evolve and adapt to new situations. It represents subconscious impulses and your ability to understand others' behavior through your intuition; it may also reveal your moral qualities. If there are several planets in this house in your birth chart, your life may be full of change.

✦ 9th House ✦

The ninth house is the House of Journeys. It refers to the impulses, aspirations, and hopes that you have for the future. It promotes your personal growth and openness toward the new and unknown—a country to visit, a language to learn—and indicates the intensity of your sense of adventure; it tells of your relationship with travel, whether real or spiritual, searching for a broadening of the conscience and a deep sense of living. It is no coincidence that it also indicates your relationship with spirituality. Check the location of Jupiter in your birth chart for further information on these aspects.

✦ 10th House ✦

The tenth house is the House of Ambition; it deals with your public reputation and place in society, in particular with your ability to obtain prestige and authority through the image of yourself that you project outward. It can indicate the level of popularity that you are able to reach and your desire to obtain recognition and success through your social standing. It also represents the qualities and aspects of yourself that are most obvious and accessible to others, as well as your relationship with authority. Take a look at the position of Saturn for more information on these subjects.

✦ 11th House ✦

The eleventh house is the House of Friendship. It indicates your relationship with friends and, in a broader sense, how you understand the concept of "belonging": to the space you leave for feelings of brother- and sisterhood and the way in which you participate and contribute to the common good, sharing ideals and hopes. If there are many planets in this house in your birth chart, you probably have an active, stimulating social life, made up of many relationships and a strong interest in humanitarian themes, a lack of preconceptions, and great magnanimity. Take a look at the position of Uranus in your birth chart for further information.

✦ 12th House ✦

The twelfth house is the House of Secrets. It is the final house, which is why it represents the dissolution of the ego. It deals with transcendence, introspection, and the spiritual evolution to which you aspire in order to free yourself from emotional scars, as well as how you deal with the painful truths that you keep hidden from yourself, how you live with your weaknesses, and how you deal with temptation. It is also associated with self-deception and illusion and indicates your relationship with reality and imagination.

The Planets

PLANET	MEANING
Sun	Personality, self, ego, sense of purpose, vitality
Moon	Emotions, intuition, feelings, instincts
Mercury	Communication, thinking, learning style
Venus	Beauty, values, love
Mars	Passion, action, strength, drive, motivation
Jupiter	Luck, expansion, belief, truth, freedom, joy, ethics
Saturn	Status, authority, parental figures, rules, limits, discipline, wisdom, ambition, patience, honor, hardships
Uranus	Originality, individuality, truth, independence, difference, sudden changes, revolution
Neptune	Dreams, illusions, psychic receptivity, uncertainty, creativity, mystery, healing, lack of boundaries
Pluto	Subconscious, personal transformation, intensity, mystery, what's below the surface, sexuality

✦ The Sun ✦

The Sun represents your personality and what makes you "you." The Sun is the center of the solar system and ourselves. Much of your personality is defined by your Sun sign, but that doesn't mean that everyone with the same Sun sign is the same. The Sun only shows a large part of who you are, deep down on the inside. It also shows how you express yourself to the world.

✦ The Moon ✦

The Moon represents your emotions, feelings, and basic needs. It's reflective, intuitive, and instinctive. It shows how you may respond to the world around you. The Moon allows you to better understand yourself and helps you peek into yourself to see how you truly feel. The Moon helps you accept yourself and become more aware.

✦ The Ascendant or Rising ✦

Your Ascendant, or Rising, sign is the zodiac sign that was rising over the eastern horizon at the time you were born, and it reveals how you like to express yourself. The Ascendant is always the beginning of your chart and is the "cusp" of the first house. This is often the mask that you choose to show to the world. It's still you, but it's how you prefer others to see you.

✦ The Descendant ✦

Your Descendant sign is directly opposite your Ascendant sign on your birth chart. It represents your rejected parts and reveals what you are attracted to. It's a good indicator of the qualities you admire and the signs you are likely compatible with.

✦ Mercury ✦

Mercury represents how you think, learn, and communicate. It designates the nature and expression of your mentality, offering insights into how you perceive reality, your intellectual abilities, your quickness of thought, and how you take on or exchange information with others.

✦ Venus ✦

Venus represents how you relate to others around you, what you value, and how you love. It is linked to the choices you make, the manner and time you employ in searching for pleasure, your need for harmony and affectionate contact with others, and how you express your love for living and what you care about.

✦ Mars ✦

Mars represents your motivation, drive, and desires. It influences the way in which you affirm yourself in the world, your capacity for fighting for the causes you believe in, and how you act and react to what happens to you. It can also indicate how aggressive and passionate you are.

Jupiter, Saturn, Uranus, Neptune, Pluto

These so-called "generational," slow, or semi-slow planets are far away from the sun, and their orbits are extremely long. This means that they remain in the same sign for a very long time, influencing and highlighting collective changes rather than the traits and characteristics of a specific personality. It takes Jupiter almost twelve years to complete an orbit around the sun; for Saturn it takes twenty-nine and a half years, Uranus eighty-four years, Neptune one hundred and sixty-four years, and Pluto two hundred and forty-eight years. Because these planets have no specific influence on birth charts, you will not find specific information on them in the following pages.

Fire signs

△

The **element of Fire** is represented by a red triangle pointing up. The zodiac signs linked to this element are **Aries** (cardinal sign dominated by Mars and corresponding to the first house), **Leo** (fixed sign dominated by the Sun and corresponding to the fifth house), and **Sagittarius** (mutable sign dominated by Jupiter and corresponding to the ninth house). Like the element to which they belong, fire signs represent desire and creative energy. They are warm, bold, and outgoing but may be overly impulsive, impatient, and as destructive as wildfire. In the zodiac circle, they are opposite and complementary to the air signs.

Aries

March 21–
April 20

A ries is the first of the twelve zodiac signs and is symbolized by the ram: strong and confident. A cardinal fire sign, Aries is known to break ground on new ideas and inspire others with its passion and desire for action. Aries rules the first house—the House of Self. In the tarot, it is represented by the Emperor card.

✦ Sun ✦

PERSONALITY AND TEMPERAMENT

You are charismatic and freedom-loving, and you feel drawn to lead the way for others to follow. When life presents you with a challenge, you likely enjoy tackling it head-on, embracing your assertive nature.

✦ Moon ✦

FEELINGS AND EMOTIONAL INTELLIGENCE

You are confident and quick to act. Your emotions are intense and passionate. You can enjoy your own company, especially when you have a problem to solve.

✦ Ascendant ✦

SOCIABILITY AND SOCIAL LIFE

You are brave and independent, enjoy new beginnings, and have creative pursuits. You like to approach life in a straightforward way and move toward your purposes without hesitation.

✦ Descendant ✦

SUBCONSCIOUS AND DEEP CONNECTIONS

You bond quickly with others through your passion and warmth. You may be impulsive and hasty with others because you are challenge-loving and always in motion.

✦ Mercury ✦

INTELLIGENCE AND COMMUNICATION SKILLS

You have an agile mind, make sharp decisions independently, and feel confident expressing yourself. You don't need to rely on others' thoughts to form your own conclusions.

✦ Venus ✦

LOVE AND DESIRE

You are authentic and honest and may initiate your relationships by being prone to moving fast. You are fueled by passion and action but still enjoy your independence.

✦ Mars ✦

ACTION AND PASSION

You are self-motivated and self-assured, taking the initiative to lead the way and remaining unwavering in your drive. You might not enjoy following another's direction.

Magic and Aries

The magical power of Aries is at its strongest during the Aries season in summer, when the sun is highest in the sky, and on Tuesday, its day of power. To tap into this fiery energy, harness the fire magic in spells and rituals on new moons to enhance your intuition.

Love

Harmonious pairing

You are best paired with another fire sign that can understand your passionate nature. While not free from challenges, these pairings are generally in harmony with each other. With an Ascendant in Aries, you're likely drawn to the qualities of a Pisces.

✦

Good pairing

The air signs can be good pairings due to their openness in communication and social nature. While not completely in harmony, these relationships may have challenges to overcome.

✦

Challenging pairing

You may face difficult connections with water signs, due to their intensity and emotions, and earth signs, due to their stubbornness and relaxed nature. These pairings have an opportunity to work through contrasting connections.

Magical tips

The tarot can give you valuable advice in deciphering your doubts about love through the images, colors, and symbolic associations present in the Major Arcana.

With the full moon in Aries, draw three cards from the deck. Each one will answer a specific question:

Card 1: What is your role in the relationship?

Card 2: What is the role of the other person in the relationship?

Card 3: How would you describe the relationship and its dynamics?

Look at the cards. Try to understand what feelings they stir in you and if they help you resolve your dilemmas.

Work

The best

Aries is a cardinal fire sign, which means that you are in-dependent and a natural-born leader. You are unafraid of tight schedules while working on a project and are always looking for a new, thrilling challenge and adrena-line rush while keeping the workflow under control. You work well with the air signs Aquarius and Gemini, due to their energy, creativity, and ability to brainstorm collec-tively to find solutions, and the fire sign Sagittarius, due to your shared drive, pursuit of new environments, and desire for exploring brand-new possibilities.

✦

Has potential

You can work well with the other fire signs—Aries and Leo—but since you all aspire to a leadership position within the team, you may face challenges when occasional power struggles manifest. You may also work well with the water signs Cancer and Pisces due to your determination and new ideas. You can help any signs put their ideas into motion.

✦

To avoid

You may struggle to overcome challenges with the earth signs—Taurus, Virgo, and Capricorn—due to their strong will and desire for long-term plans. Libra and Scorpio are other signs that may be challenging to work with: Libra can appear less serious than you on project management and deadlines, while Scorpio has a passion for putting their heart and soul into their work.

Magical tips

Tarot is a powerful tool in becoming aware of your desires and can offer interesting suggestions on questions regarding your aspirations.

Try to focus on the goal of your meditation.

1. Draw the card representing your zodiac sign; Aries is symbolized by the Emperor card.
2. Draw the card corresponding to the position of Mars in your birth chart.
3. Draw a card of your choice.

Dwell on the images of the extracted Arcana. What ideas do they evoke in you?

Family

Aries parents

Aries are very active parents, regardless of gender, and are great at establishing order and structure and encouraging sports or activities due to their inherent drive and motivation. However, Aries' tempers can flare in arguments, and they may get carried away in the heat of the moment.

Aries siblings

Being an Aries sibling means you get along well with all fire signs—Aries, Leo, and Sagittarius—because of their high energy and love of fun and the air signs Gemini and Libra because of their ability to express themselves. Capricorn also works well as a sibling due to their strong bonds and ability to plan.

Magical tips

Use the gemstones connected with your star sign to create beautiful amulets to gift to the people you love: red coral gives energy and prevents emotional imbalances; ruby symbolizes spiritual love, passion, and prosperity; red jasper instills courage and promotes physical and mental resistance; garnet helps rediscover optimism and strength to take on new challenges; and carnelian gives energy and keeps impulsivity, jealousy, and envy at bay.

Leo

July 23–
August 22

The fifth sign of the zodiac, Leo is associated with the characteristics of the animal whose name it bears: individualism, courage,
pride. The last of the fixed signs, it represents the ability to focus on oneself to achieve any goal. The height of summer is its
time, when the heat of the sun reaches its apex; for this reason, the
fire element is more evident in Leo than in other fire signs. In the
tarot, it is represented by the card of the Sun, the sign's ruling star.

✦ Sun ✦

PERSONALITY AND TEMPERAMENT

Enthusiastic and generous, you are always looking for opportunities to have fun and are energized when you are the center of attention. Don't let yourself be overshadowed! Your competitive nature may overwhelm you.

✦ Moon ✦

FEELINGS AND EMOTIONAL INTELLIGENCE

You express your emotions with passion, radiating genuine warmth. However, try to control your impulses—if someone disappoints you, you could lash out at them.

✦ Ascendant ✦

SOCIABILITY AND SOCIAL LIFE

You love to flaunt your talents in an ostentatious way. You may be afraid of not living up to others' expectations, but fear not—your positivity is contagious.

✦ Descendant ✦

SUBCONSCIOUS AND DEEP CONNECTIONS

The Ascendant in Aquarius is characterized by a strong sense of communion with the community. Your self-esteem is strengthened through encounters with your fellow humans.

✦ Mercury ✦

INTELLIGENCE AND COMMUNICATION SKILLS

With a practical and concise intelligence, you love sharing your ideas and hearing the sound of your own voice! You may be a creative and entertaining storyteller.

✦ Venus ✦

LOVE AND DESIRE

You are an overwhelming lover! A compliment is enough to get your attention. When you're in a relationship you believe in, you manage to keep your authority at bay and make loyalty a strongpoint.

✦ Mars ✦

ACTION AND PASSION

You have great fortitude, and your stubbornness and exuberance make it easy for you to assert yourself. Try to keep your pride at bay—your need for recognition could quickly lead to confrontation.

Magic
and Leo

The magical power of Leo is at its strongest during the Leo season in summer, when the sun is highest in the sky, and on Sunday, its day of power. Tap into the power and strength of fiery Leo and cast spells related to creativity, courage, strength, and power.

Love

Harmonious pairing

Fire signs are the ideal mates for you, as they appreciate your passionate spirit and impulsiveness. You may also have a great connection with air signs, as you share an outgoing soul and a desire to have fun.

✦

Good pairing

Although you have few affinities, you could form a lasting match with Taurus due to your shared desire to build a stable relationship. Compatibility is good with the water signs Cancer and Scorpio, as your need for validation and admiration compensates their search for emotional stability.

✦

Challenging pairing

Pisces' sweetness may ensnare you at first, but their sensitivity will soon bore you. Your desire for emotionally charged, theatrical gestures may not be satisfied by reserved Capricorn and down-to-earth Virgo. Best to avoid!

Magical tips

To summon the courage to find your soulmate, light a red candle on Leo's day of power: Sunday. Focus on what you desire and send your intentions out into the world. Use fire magic to help you work through challenging love situations or heartache. Write down your feelings on small pieces of paper, then pass them through the candle's flame before dropping them one at a time into a cast-iron cauldron or firesafe container. Fire is excellent for banishing all that no longer serves you.

Work

The best

Ambitious, determined, and brilliant, you are always looking for a project to believe in and in which you can express your individuality, courage, and creative passion. You have a strong charisma, which makes you an outstanding leader. Loyal Cancer, brilliant Libra, impetuous Leo, and optimistic Sagittarius appreciate your talents wholeheartedly.

✦

Has potential

Working with a Gemini might pose some challenges, but your determination can keep their lack of organization at bay. With Aries, you can choose to either clash or join your impetuous forces for excellent results. The practical sense of Capricorn and the abstract ability of Pisces can help you achieve any goal, if you combine your resources.

✦

To avoid

Your working relationship with Aquarius is decidedly complicated—you may mistake his out-of-the-box attitude for irreverence. There are many differences with Taurus and Scorpio, due to the competitive component of your signs. Virgo's perfectionism doesn't sit well with you, as you prefer to get to the goal without becoming lost in details and planning.

Magical tips

Tarot is a powerful tool in becoming aware of your desires and can offer interesting suggestions on questions regarding your aspirations.

Try to focus on the goal of your meditation.

1. Draw the card representing your zodiac sign; Leo is symbolized by the Sun card.
2. Draw the card corresponding to the position of Mars in your birth chart.
3. Draw a card of your choice.

Dwell on the images of the extracted Arcana. What ideas do they evoke in you?

Family

Leo parents

Leo parents are loving, protective, and loyal. With their courage and energy, they are the linchpin of the family and always try to keep their children's self-esteem high. They love to give lots of gifts and always find opportunities to share moments together, although they will expect to be thanked for their efforts—when they feel ignored, they may get short-tempered.

Leo siblings

Leo brothers and sisters are fun-loving and sharing, which is why they get along very well with the three fire signs. They share a strong sense of imagination with Pisces and Cancer, and together they invent fantastic worlds for their stories, in which Leo obviously takes center stage.

Magical tips

Use the gemstones connected with your star sign to create beautiful amulets to gift to the people you love: diamond symbolizes vitality, has regenerating and purifying powers, and helps overcome fear; amber instills creativity and is the stone of spontaneity, optimism, and openness toward others; and tiger's-eye helps find new balance.

Sagittarius

November 22–
December 21

Sagittarius is a mutable fire sign that lights up late autumn nights. Ruled by Jupiter, the planet of abundance and joviality, its day of the week is Thursday. His is a lightning fire, like the arrows shot by the centaur that represents him: speed of action and versatility are the characteristics of this sign. In the tarot, it is represented by the Wheel of Fortune, related to the winter solstice—the last night of Sagittarius and the darkest of the year.

✦ Sun ✦

PERSONALITY AND TEMPERAMENT

Jupiter in your sign gives you sociability and curiosity. Although you have strong principles, your changing nature can lead you to make approximate choices, but if you keep your desires in mind, any destination will be a happy one.

✦ Moon ✦

EMOTIONS AND EMOTIONAL INTELLIGENCE

You are outgoing but have a hard time hiding a decidedly restless side. Idealistic and romantic, you have an unshakable sense of justice. The fire of the sign means you are easy to ignite, but any wrong done to you is forgotten just as quickly.

✦ Ascendant ✦

SOCIABILITY AND SOCIAL LIFE

Your incurably optimistic approach and a good dose of lightheartedness allow you to face any challenge life has in store for you in the best possible way. You don't allow those who define you as naive to bring you down.

✦ Descendant ✦

SUBCONSCIOUS AND DEEP CONNECTIONS

The curiosity, quick thinking, and brilliant communication skills of a Gemini Ascendant give you a strong intuitive capacity and ability to correlate events.

✦ Mercury ✦

INTELLIGENCE AND COMMUNICATION SKILLS

You express your ideas frankly and directly, without filters or formalities. You may be accused of lacking empathy; try to weigh your words better and refine your listening skills.

✦ Venus ✦

LOVE AND DESIRE

Adventurous and exuberant, you are subject to love at first sight and brief, intense attraction. You are unable to give up freedom and variety, and you do not tolerate jealousy and routine.

✦ Mars ✦

ACTION AND PASSION

You are full of enthusiasm and like to live day-to-day, but often make hasty decisions. Learn to regulate your excess energy—pour it into planning new adventures that keep your curiosity alive.

Magic
and Sagittarius

The magical power of Sagittarius is at its strongest when the sun is high in the sky during the Sagittarius season. Cast a spell by candlelight on a Thursday to fully enjoy this sign's adventurous and enterprising nature.

Love

Harmonious pairing

It's not hard to tell when you're in love with someone—your forthright gestures leave little doubt as to your intentions. You share a passionate spirit with fire signs but try to mitigate your competitiveness. Your desire for freedom fits well with the characteristics of air signs, but try to keep jealousy at bay.

Good pairing

Although you are the most adventurous sign of the zodiac and Taurus is the most habitual, you can form an unexpected bond. The mysterious Scorpio is well able to charm you, especially during the courtship phase. The kindness of Pisces resonates with your deepest ideals; together you will know how to support each other without letting the relationship become overwhelming.

✦

Challenging pairing

You may feel stifled by sedentary Cancers—they don't like your abrupt ways and won't hide it from you! Virgos are control freaks, and you can't stand being forced to do their will. With Capricorn, friction is around the corner; their shyness is a poor match for your exuberance.

Magical tips

The waxing moon in Sagittarius is the perfect time to use the magical and seductive power of candles to access your inner world. The glow of the fire, combined with the power of this sign, will help your desires resonate throughout the universe. Find a candle—white, if possible—and in the moonlight engrave on it the name of the person you love. Concentrate your energies on your deepest desires, light the candle, say their name and then your own in a steady voice, and let the candle burn in the soft light of the moon.

Work

The best

You are well-liked for your exuberance and outspoken-ness; your fire sign colleagues can always count on you to brighten up even the dullest day. However, you must learn to keep an eye on deadlines and remember that details matter, too. Air sign colleagues are undoubtedly the most extravagant you may come across—and eccentricity is a feature that you appreciate. Join forces to get rid of antiquated and ineffective ways of working.

✦

Has potential

Try to give your water sign colleagues a chance—don't be intimidated by their reservedness, and leave the organizational part of the work in their hands while you unleash your creativity. If you work out how to make the most of your differences, you will bring interesting innovations to any creative process.

✦

To avoid

The earth signs don't appreciate your talents at all. The stubborn Taurus reproaches you for your lack of constancy—they can't hide their competitive spirit! Details and scheduling are an obstacle to your creative process, but meticulous Virgo nails you to deadlines. For Capricorn, it is essential to follow the rules; they may find your lack of diplomacy very embarrassing.

Magical tips

Tarot is a powerful tool in becoming aware of your desires and can offer interesting suggestions on questions regarding your aspirations.

Try to focus on the goal of your meditation.

1. Draw the card representing your zodiac sign; Sagittarius is symbolized by the Wheel of Fortune card.
2. Draw the card corresponding to the position of Mars in your birth chart.
3. Draw a card of your choice.

Dwell on the images of the extracted Arcana. What ideas do they evoke in you?

Family

Sagittarius parents

Like all fire signs, Sagittarius parents tend to be protective of their family, but they are not apprehensive—their greatest desire is to help their children reach their ideals and broaden their perspectives with travel and adventures full of discovery. Thanks to their unconventional ways, they know how to pass on the value of freedom in all its forms.

Sagittarius siblings

Even while quick to hand out harsh judgments, Sagittarius siblings are always quick to stand by the people they care about and love to entertain them. They are tirelessly looking for new, reckless games, and other fire signs are excellent companions in adventure. Aquarius siblings share Sagittarius' noblest ideals and passion for long speeches—best of all in a tree house!

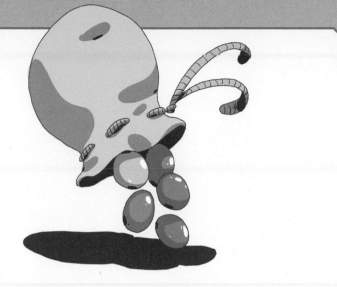

Magical tips

Use the gemstones connected with your star sign to create beautiful amulets to gift to the people you love: turquoise promotes a balance between heart and mind and helps manage stress; azurite allows decisions to be made with judgment and lucidity of thought and makes communication with others more fluid; topaz infuses positivity; zircon facilitates contact with one's roots and with a more spiritual side of existence; and tanzanite is useful for choosing between two different paths.

Earth signs

▽

The **element of earth** is represented by a green triangle pointing down. The zodiac signs linked to this element are **Taurus** (a fixed sign dominated by Venus and corresponding to the second house), **Virgo** (a mutable sign dominated by Mercury and corresponding to the sixth house), and **Capricorn** (a cardinal sign dominated by Saturn and corresponding to the tenth house). Earth signs represent property and material possessions. They are patient, tenacious, and calm but may be inflexible and stubborn. In the zodiac circle, they are opposite and complementary to the water signs.

Taurus

April 21–
May 20

The first fixed earth sign, Taurus is down-to-earth and tenacious, and has a strong sense of reality. The constellation of Taurus rises in the midspring sky, when nature is at the height of its luxuriance; unsurprisingly, the animal from which the sign gets its name has always been a symbol of fertility. It is governed by Venus, giving those born under the sign a marked aesthetic sense. In the tarot, it is represented by the Hierophant card, which symbolizes tradition and constancy.

✦ Sun ✦

PERSONALITY AND TEMPERAMENT

You are cautious and measured, and you don't like the unexpected; you plan every-thing meticulously. Despite your prudence, you are the most tenacious sign of the zodiac—when you embark on a journey, it's because you know you can make it.

✦ Moon ✦

EMOTIONS AND EMOTIONAL INTELLIGENCE

You are soft-spoken and rarely fall prey to your emotions. Your spasmodic search for stability could hide a lazy soul—learn to accommodate change.

✦ Ascendant ✦

SOCIABILITY AND SOCIAL LIFE

You have a great, vital energy that gives you an unshakable resolve. Try not to turn your tenacity into stub-bornness. Don't be too lenient with yourself, and learn to recognize when you are wrong.

✦ Descendant ✦

SUBCONSCIOUS AND DEEP CONNECTIONS

A Scorpio Ascendant is character-ized by a strong sense of empathy and emotionality, which strengthens your emotional intelligence by help-ing you understand what happens to the people you love.

✦ Mercury ✦

INTELLIGENCE AND COMMUNICATION SKILLS

You have a practical intelligence and communicate your ideas kindly but without mincing your words. You have an iron rationality, and you carefully measure what you say; you are in no hurry to express your opinion.

✦ Venus ✦

LOVE AND DESIRE

You are loyal, reliable, and passion-ate. Before starting a relationship, you consider each aspect carefully. Your need for security may also spill over into how you manage your affection, leaving you possessive and jealous.

✦ Mars ✦

ACTION AND PASSION

Mars in Taurus loses the impetuous characteristics that are typical of the planet: you face challenges with practical sense and calmness. You love peace, but your peaceful ways hide a great tenacity.

Magic
and Taurus

Taurus energy is expressed at its maximum power in spells related to stability, prosperity, and
material well-being. Use the power of the full
moon in Taurus to strengthen ties with those
closest to you, honor your feelings, and transform your home into your own little temple.

Love

Harmonious pairing

You are romantic and eager to build a stable relationship. The union is intense and lasting with earth signs. Cancer is affectionate and loyal; you will never betray each other. With Libra, another sign ruled by Venus, you share a love of beauty and a search for harmony.

✦

Good pairing

Leo offers you the protection you seek, but try not to be too stubborn. Don't be fazed by the mood swings of water signs Pisces and Scorpio—they will offer you the sensitivity you desire. Although Sagittarius clamors for their independence, you will form an unusual but strong bond.

✦

Challenging pairing

With Aries, relationships are full of unexpected events; their explosive nature collides with your rationality. Expect turbulent relationships with your air mates Gemini and Aquarius—their fickleness could trigger your jealousy.

Magical tips

Use the power of the earth element to get closer to your desires and find love again. When the new moon in Taurus shines high in the sky, collect a small pile of soil and place it in a vase. Plant a seed; you can choose from watermelon, asparagus, basil, beet and chard, artichoke, cardoon, carrot, cabbage, chicory, onion, fennel, lettuce, melon, eggplant, pepper, pea, parsley, radish, arugula, celery, or zucchini. Every time you water the plant, send happy thoughts to your loved one. The more intense the thoughts, the stronger they will reverberate throughout the universe.

Work

Work

The best

You are reliable and methodical—an excellent worker! Cooperation with earth signs always leads to excellent results. A working relationship with curious Sagittarius would be complementary; you have the tools to turn his ideas into reality. Cancer is punctual and tenacious; all your projects will be successful. You may not be as unconventional as Aquarius, but together you will develop great ideas.

✦

Has potential

Although Libra loves to wander from one project to another while you work routinely, Venus in the sign will unite you in your search for calm and harmony. Despite the mood swings and bad moods, Pisces are excellent coworkers when it comes to dealing with sudden emergencies; together you will form an excellent team.

✦

To avoid

Your competitive streak will cause difficulties when working with fire signs Aries and Leo; you will find yourselves in heated debates very easily. Geminis struggle to stay focused on a single goal, a trait that you find annoying. With Scorpio, hostilities are constantly lurking around the corner; you are very stubborn and always want to have the last word.

Magical tips

Tarot is a powerful tool in becoming aware of your desires and can offer interesting suggestions on questions regarding your aspirations.

Try to focus on the goal of your meditation.

1. Draw the card representing your zodiac sign; Taurus is symbolized by the Hierophant card.
2. Draw the card corresponding to the position of Mars in your birth chart.
3. Draw a card of your choice.

Dwell on the images of the extracted Arcana. What ideas do they evoke in you?

Family

Taurus parents

Taurus parents don't let themselves be discouraged by their children's excesses and whims; they are the most patient sign of the zodiac. They do their best to ensure that the family is built on a solid foundation and that the home is a comfortable place to spend time together. Their only flaw is that they can't stand mess!

Taurus siblings

Thanks to their calmness and discipline, Taurus brothers and sisters have the ability to quell the turmoil that often arises in the family—especially if they have overactive and messy air brothers and sisters. They rarely share their toys; they are very jealous and at times a little despotic. They have strong bonds with water signs. A warning for Scorpio brothers and sisters: to Taurus, there is no such thing as a secret!

Magical tips

Use the gemstones connected with your star sign to create beautiful amulets to gift to the people you love: emerald promotes balance, harmony, and good sense; green jade symbolizes spiritual and material wealth and protects against negative energies; green tourmaline amplifies positive vibes and aids recognition of the positive aspects of life; green aventurine eases comparisons to others; rose quartz instills romance; and fluorite helps the balance between heart and mind.

Virgo

**August 23–
September 22**

Amutable earth sign, Virgo rises in the sky at the end of summer, when the days become shorter and nature concludes its reproductive cycle: the earth has bestowed all its riches and is preparing to rest. It is therefore no surprise that those born under the sign are thrifty and responsible. Virgo is associated with the planet Mercury, representing attention to detail and reason. In the tarot, it is represented by the Hermit card, which symbolizes purity and the need to withdraw from the world to find one's balance.

✦ Sun ✦

PERSONALITY AND TEMPERAMENT

You are a perfectionist, are methodical, and have strong beliefs that you back up with logical reasoning. You have a great sense of observation—use it to understand when your desire for control becomes an obstacle.

✦ Moon ✦

EMOTIONS AND EMOTIONAL INTELLIGENCE

You are reserved and thoughtful, with a strong introspective ability. Equipped with an iron rationality, you rarely like to express your emotions. Don't let your emotional side scare you.

✦ Ascendant ✦

SOCIABILITY AND SOCIAL LIFE

One might think that you are not very spontaneous, but in truth you have a great practical sense—you never talk nonsense, and you prefer gestures over intellectual speculation. Try not to be too self-critical.

✦ Descendant ✦

SUBCONSCIOUS AND DEEP CONNECTIONS

The Ascendant in Pisces makes you empathetic and receptive to the moods of others, characteristics that lead you to do your best for others with care and foresight.

✦ Mercury ✦

INTELLIGENCE AND COMMUNICATION SKILLS

You have an analytical intelligence. Mercury in your sign gives you strong communication skills and mental clarity, a quality that allows you to analyze situations from different points of view.

✦ Venus ✦

LOVE AND DESIRE

In love, your approach is prudent and marked by realism: you demonstrate your feelings with small gestures and avoid romantic outbursts. You are looking for emotional stability and want to build a lasting relationship.

✦ Mars ✦

ACTION AND PASSION

You have a marked strategic ability, which makes you calculate the risks and dangers of every situation. Your logical approach might make you appear cold and a little aloof. You prefer farsightedness over impulse.

Magic and Virgo

Virgo energy favors spells related to health and physical well-being. The new moon in Virgo helps you focus your energies on breaking unhealthy cycles and kick-starting new, healthy habits.

Love

Harmonious pairing

With the earth signs Taurus and Capricorn, you share a need for stability and a certain calmness—fertile ground for lasting love. Cancer shares your need for security and love of routine. You may find an intense mental connection with Gemini, as long as you don't let their constant search for novelty upset you.

Good pairing

You will find a durable relationship with fellow Virgos thanks to your shared foundations, but try to leave room for improvisation if you don't want things to become monotonous. You will have a strong attraction to Pisces; his visionary nature can teach you to be less rigid. Scorpio charms you with his mysterious ways, but don't let his emotionality scare you.

Challenging pairing

Relationships with fire signs could be complicated: Leo's self-centeredness, Aries' fury, and Sagittarius' desire for freedom are difficult to reconcile with your realistic and routine nature. You will find the clash with Libra and Aquarius radical—their abstract and intuitive worldview is in stark contrast to your practical sense.

Magical tips

Sapphire is one of the gemstones of the sign of Virgo; it represents mutual understanding, loyalty, and fidelity. It is also a powerful tool in counteracting dispersion, clarifying one's heart, and focusing on necessary changes. Find somewhere you feel safe, make yourself comfortable, and try to get in touch with your deepest desires. Hold the sapphire tightly in your left hand and turn your thoughts to those you love. Say out loud first their name and then your own, so that your wishes resonate throughout the universe.

Work

The best

You are efficient and very organized, qualities that make you an irreplaceable worker. You can form an impeccable team with earth signs, as you are methodical and punctual. Fruitful collaborations can happen with Cancer and Scorpio, too: Cancer has sure-footedness and a cool head when dealing with any unexpected event, while Scorpio is meticulous and attentive to detail.

✦

Has potential

You are very rational and need stability—for you, work is essential to ensuring a dignified life and keeping you busy. Despite your differences, you can find a good balance with the air signs Gemini and Libra: Gemini can bring some verve to your professional life, while Libra shares your discreet aesthetic sense—together you can enjoy decorating the common areas with plants and imaginative objects.

✦

To avoid

Collaborating with fire signs can be tiring: Aries, Leo, and Sagittarius aren't good at meeting deadlines, which you could find annoying. Things could get complicated with Aquarius: you are attentive to detail, while Aquarius prefers to have an overview. Collaborating with Pisces could also present obstacles: you have an analytical approach, while Pisces seeks an emotional connection.

Magical tips

Tarot is a powerful tool in becoming aware of your desires and can offer interesting suggestions on questions regarding your aspirations.

Try to focus on the goal of your meditation.

1. Draw the card representing your zodiac sign; Virgo is symbolized by the Hermit card.
2. Draw the card corresponding to the position of Mars in your birth chart.
3. Draw a card of your choice.

Dwell on the images of the extracted Arcana. What ideas do they evoke in you?

Family

Virgo parents

Virgo parents are responsible and practical. They are quite reserved and do not like to give compliments; they show their affection by showering their children with gifts and do their best to offer their family a high standard of living. However, they are very demanding, and it can be easy to disappoint them.

Virgo siblings

Virgo brothers and sisters feel very protective of their family, although it's something they rarely demonstrate with words. Their bond is strong with earth signs: they are practical and commonsense playmates, and they have fun completing a puzzle or playing a board game together. With a Scorpio brother or sister, competition coupled with the common pursuit of perfection will lead to some increasingly complex pastimes.

Magical tips

Use the gemstones connected with your star sign to create beautiful amulets to gift to the people you love: pearl helps to release emotions; sapphire symbolizes truth and constancy and is useful in strengthening mutual understanding and a sense of loyalty; carnelian gives vitality, drives away negative feelings, and favors relationships with others; amethyst infuses serenity and balance; rose quartz helps with opening up to others and gives practical sense and lucidity of thought; and red jasper promotes concentration.

Capricorn

December 22– January 20

The last cardinal earth sign, Capricorn welcomes the winter solstice, when days start to grow longer and nature prepares itself against the cold. Capricorn is the sign of solid, stubborn people; the goat that represents it is in fact able to reach the very highest heights. It is governed by Saturn, which gives those born under this sign strength of character and resilience but also a melancholic temperament. In the tarot, it is associated with the arcane Devil, a card of introspection and psychological investigation.

✦ Sun ✦

PERSONALITY AND TEMPERAMENT

You are the most reflective sign of the zodiac. You are not guided impetuously but rather by patience and dedication to the causes you believe in. You love solitude and may seem cold and detached; never be afraid to show your vulnerable side.

✦ Moon ✦

EMOTIONS AND EMOTIONAL INTELLIGENCE

You are thoughtful and aware of your needs. Despite the confidence and emotional detachment you show, you hide a sensitive soul that manifests when the sentiments in play are deep.

✦ Ascendant ✦

SOCIABILITY AND SOCIAL LIFE

You prefer concreteness to daydreams and are gifted with a great practical sense. Because you are aware of your tenacity and discipline, you like taking on responsibilities.

✦ Descendant ✦

SUBCONSCIOUS AND DEEP CONNECTIONS

A Cancer Ascendant gives you a gentle soul and marked sense of listening, helping you find in others the support and motivation you use to gather the fruits of your efforts.

✦ Mercury ✦

INTELLIGENCE AND COMMUNICATION SKILLS

You tend to be taciturn, but you communicate your ideas with calm and rigor, without ever being superficial. Your judgments are clear; you can be excessively inflexible and are not inclined to consider the emotional side of situations.

✦ Venus ✦

LOVE AND DESIRE

You are private and do not particularly enjoy showing your emotions. You evaluate every detail very carefully before embarking on a relationship. You like to plan the future and want a long-lasting relationship characterized by reciprocal responsibility.

✦ Mars ✦

ACTION AND PASSION

The aggressiveness of Mars unites with the tenaciousness and ambition of the Capricorn sign. Your energy is guided by logic and pragmatism; you are oriented toward concrete choices that you will reach thanks to your sense of initiative.

Magic and Capricorn

The full moon in Capricorn helps you focus your energies to find new solutions to old problems, reflect on your accomplishments, and refine the processes you've been through to get there.

Love

Love

Harmonious pairing

Earth signs are your most kindred companions: Taurus can teach you the art of light-
ness, a union with Virgo is all about passion,
and a fellow Capricorn will share your secretive-
ness. With Cancer, the emotional understanding is perfect.

✦

Good pairing

You find air signs fun to be around, but their tendency to trust intuition and quickness of thought makes intellectual exchanges tiring. The water signs Scorpio and
Pisces are able to breach your impenetrable emotional sphere, but you will become
easily annoyed by Scorpio's touchiness and Pisces' dreamer spirit.

✦

Challenging pairing

Compatibility with fire signs is difficult: Aries loves improvisation, but you are
methodical and cautious; Leo constantly needs attention, but you hate showing
your emotions; Sagittarius likes looking for new things, but you desire calm
and stability.

Magical tips

The full moon in Capricorn is the perfect time to cast this simple spell and attract love into your life. Gather three black candles, a clove of garlic, and a picture of your loved one. Look for a green corner where you feel comfortable. Once you are ready, start meditating on the power of love and its different manifestations. Light the three candles and gaze at the image in your hands. Try to focus on the happiness of the person to whom you are addressing your invocation. Take the garlic clove and light it with the flame of the central candle, then bury it in the ground.

Work

The best

You are ambitious and excellent at managing your responsibilities; work is where you excel. You share willpower and constancy with earth signs: Taurus may show you when to take a break from your work and make time for something else; Virgo is always punctual with deadlines; and Capricorn is determined and inflexible. An affinity is also guaranteed with water signs: Cancer can teach you how to work in a team; Scorpio is very reserved; and Pisces' creative flow can feed your imagination.

✦

Has potential

Libra's frivolousness may not match with your serious and composed vision of work, but you have much to learn from each other. Leo shares your desire for success, though you take very different paths to get there; you could become an excellent team if only you could smooth out your differences.

✦

To avoid

Aries is curt and direct in manner, leaving you speechless—let them deal with the aspects of work that require a good dose of aggressiveness. Sagittarius' relaxed, cheeky behavior irritates you; don't forget that both they and Aries are fire signs. The air signs Aquarius and Gemini are not the best work companions for you: Aquarius is easily distracted, making it impossible to manage a project together, and Gemini will do everything possible to avoid repetitive tasks.

Magical tips

Tarot is a powerful tool in becoming aware of your desires and can offer interesting suggestions on questions regarding your aspirations.

Try to focus on the goal of your meditation.

1. Draw the card representing your zodiac sign; Capricorn is symbolized by the Devil card.
2. Draw the card corresponding to the position of Mars in your birth chart.
3. Draw a card of your choice.

Dwell on the images of the extracted Arcana. What ideas do they evoke in you?

Family

Capricorn parents

Capricorn parents base their educational model on order and discipline. They have a lot of ambition for their children, to whom they communicate with measured detachment, never giving in to outbursts of emotion. Thanks to a very strong sense of responsibility, they are able to give their children a lot of freedom. It is important not to test the limits imposed by their good sense—they do not tolerate disobedience and they demand respect.

Capricorn siblings

Capricorn siblings are taciturn and solitary figures. Mild-mannered and generous of heart, they try to transmit their tenacity to their brothers and sisters. They prefer games in which they can learn new things rather than games of invention. They have strong connections with Cancer siblings, but there will be no hugging or touchy-feely shows of love—they hate physical displays of affection!

Magical tips

Use the gemstones connected with your star sign to create beautiful amulets to gift to the people you love: black onyx absorbs negative energies; jade promotes communication and lucidity of thought, instills courage, and helps with self-expression; black tourmaline helps recognize mistakes and draw useful lessons from them for the future; and smoky quartz reduces fear and stress and facilitates introspection.

Air signs

The **element of Air** is represented by a yellow triangle pointing up and crossed by a horizontal line. The zodiac signs linked to this element are **Gemini** (a mutable sign dominated by Mercury and corresponding to the third house), **Libra** (a cardinal sign dominated by Venus and corresponding to the seventh house), and **Aquarius** (a fixed sign dominated by Uranus and corresponding to the eleventh house). Air signs represent intellect and communication skills. They are imaginative, lighthearted, and quick-thinking but lack practical sense. In the zodiac circle, they are opposite and complementary to the fire signs.

Gemini

May 21–
June 21

The first mutable air sign, Gemini is lively and outgoing. Its con-stellation shines in the sky at the end of spring and heralds the summer period, when a newly fertile nature prepares to bear her fruits. Gemini is dominated by Mercury, so it's no coincidence that those born under this sign have a strong communicative ability and are not afraid of change. In the tarot, it is represented by the Lovers card, which symbolizes the sacredness of communication.

✦ Sun ✦

PERSONALITY AND TEMPERAMENT

Curious, energetic, and hyperactive, you are constantly on the lookout for new stimuli; no detail escapes you. You adapt easily to any situation, but your eclecticism could lead to superficiality—don't be afraid of boredom.

✦ Moon ✦

EMOTIONS AND EMOTIONAL INTELLIGENCE

Your multiple interests and fervent imagination mean you are constantly jumping from one thought to another; your emotions arise from intellectual stimuli. You may find it hard to get in touch with your deepest feelings.

✦ Ascendant ✦

SOCIABILITY AND SOCIAL LIFE

You are versatile, acute, and lively. Your need to share is irrepressible; socializing recharges your energy, and you enjoy being around people. Thanks to your magnetic talkativeness, you always know how to entertain those around you.

✦ Descendant ✦

SUBCONSCIOUS AND DEEP CONNECTIONS

The Ascendant in Sagittarius gives you a great sense of freedom, passion, open-mindedness, and enthusiasm. Gemini's communicativeness pushes you to share your noblest intentions with as many people as possible.

✦ Mercury ✦

INTELLIGENCE AND COMMUNICATION SKILLS

Brilliant and self-confident, Gemini has the best communication skills in the zodiac. You think quickly and have a lucid intelligence and a good dose of self-irony. With your great love of rhetoric, you manage to get the better of every conversation.

✦ Venus ✦

LOVE AND DESIRE

You search for sentimental flings that can provide you with mental harmony. Your ideal partner knows how to entertain you with coherent dialogue and continuous stimuli, never boring you. For you, love is a fun game that is constantly changing over time.

✦ Mars ✦

ACTION AND PASSION

You defend your ideas with sarcasm, wit, and irrepressible frankness, often for the very pleasure of starting a debate. But be careful: you risk losing yourself in the many (too many) interests you have and could become restless and distracted.

Magic
and Gemini

The new moon is the best time to cast spells related to new beginnings. With the new moon in Gemini, you can cast spells on the success of fortune-telling and prophecy, and invoke good luck in everything to do with communication and study.

Love

Harmonious pairing

You can have lots of fun with Leo and Sagittarius: these are light relationships, full of playful bickering. Biting irony is your weapon to overcome any problem. You have an exceptional understanding with the air signs Libra and Aquarius. You like sharing thoughts and curiosities; yours is a purely mental understanding. You can establish an unusual but intense bond with Virgo. They use their confidence to seduce you and win you over.

✦

Good pairing

Aries' assertiveness might annoy you, but their vitality will make amends for any excess. Capricorn is reserved and prudent, but if your confidence does not fill them with distrust, they will fill you with their sensitivity and wisdom. With a Gemini, you risk being overwhelmed with wasted words, but you are guaranteed to have exhilarating moments together sharing the interests that most amuse you. Cancer is able to see your deepest emotional side despite your differences.

✦

Challenging pairing

The water signs Scorpio and Pisces are too sensitive for you—they are looking for emotional understanding rather than mental complicity, which for you is a vital property in any relationship; your tireless sociability could also make them feel neglected. Taurus is the most possessive and routine-loving sign of the zodiac—they love spending time at home, sharing their most intimate thoughts with you alone. You may feel trapped!

Magical tips

The power of plants can help you connect with the deepest desires residing in your heart. Get five sunflowers, a yellow ribbon, and a jar of honey. Find a place where you feel at ease. Get into a comfortable position and close your eyes. Try connecting to a thought that makes you happy, then focus on the person you love. Open your eyes and keep turning your thoughts to happiness and love as you tie the yellow ribbon around the sunflowers. Use your finger to brush honey on the sunflowers and then place them in a ceramic vase in the moonlight.

Work

The best

Your best gift is undoubtedly the ability to reason broadly on any topic without preconceptions. Your excellent communication skills make you an indispensable colleague. The air signs Libra and Aquarius know how to understand and implement your ideas, even the most pioneering ones, while the impetuous spirit of initiative from the fire signs Aries and Sagittarius can transform them into reality.

Has potential

You value Virgos for their meticulousness, but their penchant for punctuality risks interrupting your creative flow. Leo is an individualist, but their resourcefulness coupled with your quick thinking can benefit both of you. Pisces is often lazy but can also be decidedly creative—join forces if you want to realize the most original ideas. Any partnership with Cancer may have some setbacks, but from their place in the shadows, they just may amaze you with their brilliant intuition.

To avoid

For you, the best way to work is through a quick exchange of ideas. You may find communicating with fellow earth signs Taurus and Capricorn tiring: you're rarely on the same page, and you risk losing your train of thought if you have to wait for them to take part in group discussions. Scorpio doesn't play along if you want to use a joke to bring some fun to the workplace; they may annoy you with their scathing replies. It is difficult to collaborate with Geminis; together you are often inconclusive.

Magical tips

Tarot is a powerful tool in becoming aware of your desires and can offer interesting suggestions on questions regarding your aspirations.

Try to focus on the goal of your meditation.

1. Draw the card representing your zodiac sign; Gemini is symbolized by the Lovers card.
2. Draw the card corresponding to the position of Mars in your birth chart.
3. Draw a card of your choice.

Dwell on the images of the extracted Arcana. What ideas do they evoke in you?

Family

Gemini parents

Lively and communicative, Gemini parents establish an equal and friendly relationship with their children; they are always available for dialogue and ready to offer explanations for any doubt or curiosity. They want to equip their children with the intellectual tools necessary to understand the world around them and to know how to extricate themselves from a difficult situation. They love to fill family life with fun and stimulating activities. Warning: they can at times be a little indiscreet!

Gemini siblings

Gemini siblings are the perfect companions for excursions. Their voracious curiosity leads them to always explore new places for their adventures, joined by as many people as possible: brothers, sisters, or friends—the more, the better! Their perfect siblings are lively fire signs, but for Gemini, it's all about having company. And if you want to surprise them with a gift, give them a good book.

Magical tips

Use the gemstones connected with your star sign to create beautiful amulets to gift to the people you love: topaz symbolizes courage and wisdom and helps regain good humor and assert one's authority, giving optimism and energy; citrine allows ideas and projects to be transformed into useful actions, influences ideas and intelligence, and stimulates memory.

Libra

September 23–
October 22

Libra is a cardinal air sign that shines in the sky starting from the autumn equinox, when the days are equally split between light and darkness; it is no coincidence that those born under this sign are constantly searching for balance and equilibrium. Ruled by Venus, Libras have a strong aesthetic sense, elegance, and a touch of vanity. In the tarot, it is represented by the card of Justice, who holds a scale in her hands and symbolizes fairness and harmony.

✦ Sun ✦

PERSONALITY AND TEMPERAMENT

You are kind, sincere, and unconventional; if a rule doesn't work, you prefer to break it and reformulate it. While you're always ready to fight for a good cause, you rarely succumb to rage—your best weapon is diplomacy.

✦ Moon ✦

EMOTIONS AND EMOTIONAL INTELLIGENCE

You experience your emotions intensely but do not let them overwhelm you; you know how to elaborate them in a rational and balanced way. Your sense of justice gives you great empathy toward others, and you are an excellent listener.

✦ Ascendant ✦

SOCIABILITY AND SOCIAL LIFE

Optimistic and sociable, you love sharing your many interests with as many people as possible. You build new relationships easily thanks to your sincerity and kindness, which make you a valued friend.

✦ Descendant ✦

**SUBCONSCIOUS AND DEEP
CONNECTIONS**

The Ascendant in Aries gives you an incurable trust and sense of initiative, which you bestow on others with your polite ways, thanks to your ability to cooperate.

✦ Mercury ✦

**INTELLIGENCE AND
COMMUNICATION SKILLS**

Soft-spoken and sober, you avoid conflict at all costs. You use your intuition to engage in conversations marked by kindness and empathy. You have a great awareness of others, and you always know how to put them at ease.

✦ Venus ✦

LOVE AND DESIRE

You are extremely romantic—for you, love is a fundamental component of your search for equilibrium. Your strong aesthetic sense and idealism lead you to be very demanding; don't let yourself be discouraged by your fear of choosing.

✦ Mars ✦

ACTION AND PASSION

You prefer dialogue and kindness to action and aggression. Your deep desire for harmony and your tireless sense of justice lead you to use diplomacy when dealing with any situation.

Magic
and Libra

With the full moon in Libra, the time is right to
tap into the sign's harmonious energy and focus
your energies by asking yourself where in your
life you need more balance.

Love

Harmonious pairing

Your affinity with air signs Aquarius and Gemini is excellent: your communication skills allow you to achieve an intense mental connection. Despite your desire for balance, you are not afraid of being impetuous in love—you are turned on by the instinctiveness of Leo and Sagittarius. Your search for harmony and love of beautiful things is shared with the Venusian Taurus.

✦

Good pairing

Aries has a fiery manner, but your willingness to compromise may strike a satisfying balance. Cancer's sensitivity attracts you, but you shouldn't let his laziness over-whelm you. Capricorn also wants a stable relationship, but you have a hard time getting into his emotional sphere. Relationships with fellow Libras are tiring; despite your affinities, indecision could make communication complicated.

✦

Challenging pairing

It's impossible for you to get along with a Virgo; you'll be crushed by their obsession with rules. Water signs Scorpio and Pisces find you insensitive; their constant need for attention and sudden mood swings may tire you. It's best to avoid them—don't deny yourself the freedom you will find in an equal and independent relationship!

Magical tips

Friday is the best day to tap into the power of Libra. Look for somewhere you can concentrate your energies and prepare yourself with a sincere and serene soul to reflect on the characteristics you are looking for in a romantic relationship. Jot them down on a sheet of paper, then fold the sheet and squeeze it between your palms. Join your hands at heart level; try to visualize what you wrote and continue to focus on your desires, immersing yourself in the sensations you feel and the images that this short meditation has generated in your heart.

Work

The best

You like working in a team, and your search for harmony makes you a likable and appreciated colleague. Your ideal colleagues are air signs; you share their quick thinking and intuition, ensuring that you can perform any task together with fun and ease. You have no disdain for success, so the brilliant fire signs Sagittarius and Leo are your ideal allies in achieving any goal with grit and determination.

✦

Has potential

Earth signs can prove to be challenging colleagues to work with: they demand punctuality, seriousness, and discipline. However, if you work out a good compromise, you will find that each of you has a lot to learn from the other. Pisces' indecision collides with yours—you struggle to be decisive and fail to motivate yourself—but you share a keen sense of abstraction that helps you manage any creative process.

✦

To avoid

You will never get along with Aries—their arrogance is a serious problem for you, and you will try anything to avoid the direct confrontations they long for. You consider the water signs Scorpio and Cancer passive-aggressive; for their part, they don't appreciate your joviality and are confused by your constant changes of course on the decisions you make.

Magical tips

Tarot is a powerful tool in becoming aware of your desires and can offer interesting suggestions on questions regarding your aspirations.

Try to focus on the goal of your meditation.

1. Draw the card representing your zodiac sign; Libra is symbolized by the Justice card.
2. Draw the card corresponding to the position of Mars in your birth chart.
3. Draw a card of your choice.

Dwell on the images of the extracted Arcana. What ideas do they evoke in you?

Family

Libra parents

With their strong sense of ethics and sharp sensitivity, Libra parents cannot bear confrontation and do not believe in authoritarian ways and hierarchies; they establish an equal relationship with their children, in the name of calm and sincere dialogue, and safeguard the family union at all costs. For them, the home is a calm place in which they surround themselves with beautiful things and bring the family together.

Libra siblings

Mild, generous, and approachable, Libra siblings are the most thoughtful of the zodiac. They cannot tolerate controversy, which often leads them to assume the role of mediator when misunderstandings arise in the family, especially if they have fire brothers and sisters. They don't like competitive games. It's better to offer them an exhibition or a walk in nature; they appreciate company and love beauty in all its forms.

Magical tips

Use the gemstones connected with your star sign to create beautiful amulets to gift to the people you love: lapis lazuli helps balance energies; blue crystal promotes awareness of self and others; opal favors change and is useful for rediscovering optimism; malachite helps manage fears for the future and abandon the traumas of the past; and chrysoprase promotes a positive outlook on life.

Aquarius

January 21–
February 19

The final fixed air sign, Aquarius is eccentric and restless. Its constellation shines in the freezing winter sky, when the cold season reaches its peak and the air is thin. It is governed by Uranus, the planet of genius and recklessness, giving those born under the sign a brilliant mind, sharp inventiveness, high ideals, and a sense of brotherhood. In the tarot, it is represented by the Star card, symbolizing optimism and fulfillment.

✦ Sun ✦

PERSONALITY AND TEMPERAMENT

You are an unpredictable idealist, constantly searching for originality and cultivating a fervent imagination. It's difficult to harness yourself to established definitions; you can't stand strict rules and conformity. Don't let those who define you as childish bring you down.

✦ Moon ✦

EMOTIONS AND EMOTIONAL INTELLIGENCE

You have excellent intuition; your first impressions are rarely wrong. You have deep beliefs in freedom, and your open-mindedness frees you from the passions that bind you. You may find it difficult to express your emotions calmly.

✦ Ascendant ✦

SOCIABILITY AND SOCIAL LIFE

You are outgoing, independent, and courageous, and you are moved by a humanitarian spirit. You are passionately dedicated to the causes close to your heart, especially if shared by others. Friendship and brotherhood are vital.

✦ Descendant ✦

SUBCONSCIOUS AND DEEP CONNECTIONS

The Ascendant in Leo gives you charisma and joviality, making it easier for you to socialize. Your wish is to meet as many people as possible and be committed to building a community that shares the very noblest of your ideals.

✦ Mercury ✦

INTELLIGENCE AND COMMUNICATION SKILLS

Yours is a very quick, intuitive intelligence. You are often restless and may seem annoyed; you need to feed your curiosity and be constantly stimulated. You may have a hard time changing your mind. Try not to get overwhelmed by idealism.

✦ Venus ✦

LOVE AND DESIRE

You are unpredictable and inconsistent, and you do not tolerate regularity at all. In love, you appreciate those who offer you variety and freedom; you are looking for a deep friendship and fervent mental exchange of original ideas and fun.

✦ Mars ✦

ACTION AND PASSION

Enthusiastic, audacious, and rebellious, you are a fierce defender of freedom in all its forms; your favorite weapons are dialogue and spontaneity. Your inconstancy could lead you away from your goals—try to develop your concentration skills through meditation.

Magic and Aquarius

The new moon in Aquarius lends huge power to spells aimed at the community. The magical power of the sign also expresses itself well in the breaking of spells, but in this case, it is better to wait for the waning moon.

Love

Love

Harmonious pairing

You are the most unpredictable and enigmatic sign of the zodiac. Your ideal companions are the air signs Libra and Gemini, as they share your carefreeness, inspiration, and passion for long chats. Your elusiveness unleashes the desire for conquest in fiery fire signs Sagittarius and Leo, and you are captivated by their charisma and effortless sociability.

Good pairing

Aries can be a lively partner, but you have to learn to put your ego aside. Capricorn offers you stability and calm, as long as they can put their jealousy aside. The understanding is intense with another Aquarius, but the relationship may take a decidedly turbulent turn. Pisces seduces you with their romantic idealism, but try to keep your feet on the ground!

Challenging pairing

The characteristics of the earth signs Taurus and Virgo are too incompatible with your ideals: they can't stand your ramblings and are extremely jealous. It doesn't bode much better with the water signs Cancer and Scorpio; you don't understand their mood swings, and their demand to share every single thing makes you feel caged.

Magical tips

The full moon in Aquarius is a great time to prepare a tea with few ingredients and focus your thoughts on your loved one.
You will need:
– 1 tablespoon spearmint
– 1 tablespoon lemon balm
– 1 tablespoon chamomile
– 1 teaspoon hawthorn leaves and flowers
– 1 teaspoon meadowsweet
– 1 teaspoon dog rose
– 1 teapot
– 1 teacup
Using your right hand, mix the herbs in a bowl, focusing your energy on the one you love. Cover the herbs with boiling water and let them steep for ten minutes. Serve the mixture and sweeten it with honey or sugar, if desired.

Work

The best

You believe that work must also have an ethical purpose and are committed to finding a meaning to transcend banality in any project. Air sign colleagues Libra and Gemini share this aspiration with you, and your shared admirable intuition and ability for abstraction mean that you will make every proposal special. When inventiveness is scarce, the charisma of your fire sign colleague Sagittarius can encourage and motivate you.

✦

Has potential

Earth sign colleagues Taurus and Capricorn know you struggle to meet deadlines, but they need your out-of-the-box creativity to set their proposals in motion and streamline the creative process. Don't expect clear and effective communication from water sign colleagues Cancer and Pisces; however, you will find them always ready to dispense emotional encouragement when motivation is running dry.

✦

To avoid

You will find it impossible to complete any tasks with an Aquarius; you would do better with a more productive sign to support you. You can't stand Leo's individualism—if there's a common victory to celebrate, they will take all the credit. It is hard to come to an agreement with a Virgo; their demand for punctuality unnerves you and turns you off. Fixed Scorpio shares your discrete rigidity, so you are unlikely to reach a compromise.

Magical tips

Tarot is a powerful tool in becoming aware of your desires and can offer interesting suggestions on questions regarding your aspirations.

Try to focus on the goal of your meditation.

1. Draw the card representing your zodiac sign; Aquarius is symbolized by the Star card.
2. Draw the card corresponding to the position of Mars in your birth chart.
3. Draw a card of your choice.

Dwell on the images of the extracted Arcana. What ideas do they evoke in you?

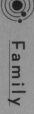

Family

Family

Aquarius parents

Aquarius parents are the most progressive of the zodiac; they want to raise their children in freedom, in the name of nonconformism. Their educational model is based on dialogue and sharing; they love organizing family reunions in a tent pitched in the garden or planning long trips in a camper van, where they enjoy entertaining the family with their bizarre stories.

Aquarius siblings

Aquarius siblings are free spirits. You may at times find it difficult to follow their reasoning or understand their choices, but they are always guided by strong ideals and a deep sense of brotherhood. They can appear a little distracted, especially to emotional water signs, but they're probably just lost in thought! A walk in nature will undoubtedly make them happy.

Magical tips

Use the gemstones connected with your star sign to create beautiful amulets to gift to the people you love: rock
crystal favors emotional stability and promotes introspection; blue sapphire helps to sort out ideas and achieve
any goal; turquoise facilitates the development of feelings
and a sense of forgiveness; and aquamarine promotes
using reason to find the best solutions.

Water signs

▽

The **element of Water** is represented by a blue triangle pointing down. The zodiac signs linked to this element are **Cancer** (a cardinal sign dominated by the Moon and corresponding to the fourth house), **Scorpio** (a fixed sign dominated by Pluto and corresponding to the eighth house), and **Pisces** (a mutable sign dominated by Neptune and corresponding to the twelfth house). Water signs represent imagination and feelings. They are receptive, empathetic, and intuitive but may be overly mysterious and impenetrable. In the zodiac circle, they are opposite and complementary to the earth signs.

Cancer

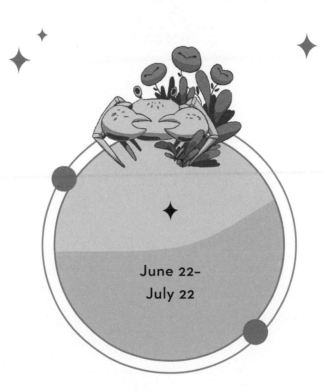

**June 22–
July 22**

The first cardinal water sign, Cancer is the dreamer of the zodiac. It is connected to the notion of emotional nourishment: the sun's entry into the constellation coincides with the summer solstice, heralding the season of ripening fruits. It is governed by the Moon, which represents the twenty-eight-day cycle of motherhood and fertility and gives those born under this sign emotional depth, moodiness, and a tendency toward melancholy. In the tarot, it is represented by the Arcanum of the Moon, symbolizing intuition and memory.

✦ Sun ✦

PERSONALITY AND TEMPERAMENT

You have a complex and mysterious personality, the gift of intuition, and remarkable emotional intelligence. Your extraordinary memory causes you to be particularly attached to the past. Your extreme sensitivity may make you shy or aggressive; don't be afraid to open up.

✦ Moon ✦

EMOTIONS AND EMOTIONAL INTELLIGENCE

The Moon is at home in your sign. You have great emotional intelligence, which means that you are quick to catch on to the moods of the people around you, with no need for words. You may be prone to sudden mood swings and paranoid thinking.

✦ Ascendant ✦

SOCIABILITY AND SOCIAL LIFE

You don't like confusion or being the center of attention; you love spending your time at home or in safe places where you feel at ease. You prefer to cultivate few but deep and lasting friendships. Try to distinguish your desire for comfort from fear.

✦ Descendant ✦

SUBCONSCIOUS AND DEEP CONNECTIONS

You seek a connection with others through your emotional vulnerability; expressing your feelings helps you find a deep serenity and experience a sense of intimate belonging to the world.

✦ Mercury ✦

INTELLIGENCE AND COMMUNICATION SKILLS

You have a sensitive intelligence and a remarkable imagination. Your thoughts are guided more by emotions than by rationality. You like daydreaming and are sensitive to the power of suggestion; be careful not to stray too far from reality.

✦ Venus ✦

LOVE AND DESIRE

You don't like flings. You are searching for security and intimacy so you can open up and show your innermost feelings. You may be moody and a little capricious.

✦ Mars ✦

ACTION AND PASSION

Mars in Cancer loses its warlike charge, and its influences are limited. You are moody and vulnerable, prone to sweetness and romance. Your aggression is not expressed directly but rather through actions of passive resistance.

Magic and Cancer

The power of this water element favors love and friendship spells. The full moon in Cancer supports you in spells to increase love toward yourself and the people you care about. The waning moon helps smooth out emotional chaos and purifies and protects the home.

Love

Harmonious pairing

You are attentive, fragile, and very romantic. The three earth signs are your closest companions: their stability and concreteness help you feel secure and ease your mood swings; you share traditional values and a love of domesticity. You have an intense affinity with Pisces, fueled by your daydreams; you are attentive and capable of grasping the innumerable nuances of your emotions.

✦

Good pairing

Although water is your element, your relationship with Scorpios and other Cancers can have some setbacks: you may feel overwhelmed by each other's emotional swings, but your inclination to listen helps you find a satisfactory understanding. Air signs Libra and Gemini don't allow much room for your sensitivity, but their playful ways manage to ease your saddest thoughts. Leo is vain, but his confidence wins you over.

✦

Challenging pairing

Aquarius is decidedly elusive and emotionally unavailable, as well as overly outgoing, sociable, and dynamic; your differences are so numerous that you will inevitably end up arguing. It's best to avoid fire signs Aries and Sagittarius—they make you nervous with their aggressive and dismissive ways, and they are not interested in emotional life, much less in daydreaming.

Magical tips

Moonstone is one of Cancer's birthstones. Linked to the water element, the moon, and the generating forces of nature, it can intensify your feelings and help you understand your deepest emotions. Find somewhere you feel safe—it can be a garden or your room—and try to get in touch with your desires. Hold the moonstone tightly in your left hand as you think with intensity and positive energy about your loved one. Say out loud first their name and then your own, so your wishes resonate throughout the universe.

Work

The best

Your receptivity to the moods of others leads you to desire a work environment in which relationships are calm and peaceful. With their composed ways, earth signs are your ideal colleagues: Taurus shares your calmness in managing emergencies, Virgo shares your meticulousness, and Capricorn shares your loyalty toward commitments. Surprisingly, Leo's authoritative strength can help you get out of emotional obstacles.

✦

Has potential

Aries and Sagittarius have brusque manners and tend to take control of situations. This doesn't necessarily represent a problem—if you think they're up to it, you don't mind caving a little and putting yourself at the service of their ideas. You have a good emotional understanding with Gemini, but their constant rambling defocuses you. With Cancer, you have unity of purpose but may lack a common drive in problem-solving.

✦

To avoid

You will find working with air sign colleagues Libra or Aquarius very complicated. You have a decidedly different approach to commitment: by their logic, they will get you to move from one project to the next without stopping, distracting you from finishing the job you started. It's strange to say, but things aren't much better with your water sign colleagues Scorpio and Pisces: your extreme sensitivity makes any interaction complex, leading to misunderstandings in communication.

Magical tips

Tarot is a powerful tool in becoming aware of your desires and can offer interesting suggestions on questions regarding your aspirations.

Try to focus on the goal of your meditation.

1. Draw the card representing your zodiac sign; Cancer is symbolized by the Moon card.
2. Draw the card corresponding to the position of Mars in your birth chart.
3. Draw a card of your choice.

Dwell on the images of the extracted Arcana. What ideas do they evoke in you?

Family

Cancer parents

Kind and loving, Cancer parents build their educational model around the idea of empathy. Thanks to their emotional intelligence, they know how to take care of their children, especially when they are very young. They show their love and cherish family memories by sharing old anecdotes; their drawers are full of photographs and relics from the past.

Cancer siblings

Cancer brothers and sisters have a visceral and protective relationship with their family members. Despite their shyness, they are tender and loving and don't mind displays of affection; air and water signs get along best with them. They may need to spend some time alone, perhaps under a tent built with blankets, where they can read and get lost in their daydreams.

Magical tips

Use the gemstones connected with your star sign to create beautiful amulets to gift to the people you love: pearl helps release emotions; moonstone strengthens personality and bonds with others; rock crystal relieves tension and calms the soul; ruby favors physical activity and relieves laziness; and emerald helps strengthen love for one's neighbor.

Scorpio

October 23–
November 21

A fixed water sign, Scorpio is enigmatic and endowed with an intense, mostly hidden emotional charge. When its constellation shines in the winter sky, the sun continues its descent into darkness and nature decomposes and retreats, awaiting regeneration. Scorpio is associated with the concept of death and rebirth. It is ruled by Mars, which conveys willpower, combativeness, ingenuity, and a certain amount of aggression. In the tarot, it is represented by the Card with No Name, the most misunderstood of the Major Arcana, a symbol of the cyclical nature of life, of change and regeneration.

✦ Sun ✦

PERSONALITY AND TEMPERAMENT

Difficult to decipher, you are the most mysterious sign of the zodiac; you tend to avoid showing your true self in order to protect your fragile emotional world. You have great intuitive skills but allow few people to get to know you. You use sarcasm as a defense.

✦ Moon ✦

EMOTIONS AND EMOTIONAL INTELLIGENCE

You have a complex emotional life. Although you are decidedly restless, you tend to hide your aggression and deepest feelings behind a calm appearance. Don't be afraid of losing control of your emotions.

✦ Ascendant ✦

SOCIABILITY AND SOCIAL LIFE

There is something magnetic about you, which means that you rarely pass unnoticed. Your harshness may inspire a certain fear; you need time to open up, which is why you prefer to choose the people you surround yourself with carefully.

✦ Descendant ✦

SUBCONSCIOUS AND DEEP CONNECTIONS

You believe in the value of simplicity. Meeting others helps you understand the world of emotions and grasp the dynamics of the unconscious.

✦ Mercury ✦

INTELLIGENCE AND COMMUNICATION SKILLS

You have a thoughtful and profound intelligence and a remarkable intuitive strength. You are an excellent listener and know how to grasp the nuances of every situation, especially the less obvious ones. You charm and convince others with ease, but you may have a tendency to be ambiguous or omit information.

✦ Venus ✦

LOVE AND DESIRE

Your love life is passionate and intense. You are magnetically attracted to unusual and complicated situations, and you enjoy the game of seduction. But when it comes to taking the next step, you tread warily. Don't be afraid to show your feelings.

✦ Mars ✦

ACTION AND PASSION

Your energy is powerful, reasoned, and effective, but what you do to achieve your goals may seem incomprehensible to others. Your passions are intense, and you are not afraid of danger; your argumentative nature may make you a brawler.

Magic and Scorpio

The magical power of Scorpio is at its strongest through the ability to be vulnerable and deep. The waning moon in Scorpio helps you cast self-defense and protection spells to purge the negativity from any situation.

Love

Love

Harmonious pairing

You search for relationships with a high emotional intensity in which you can bare your most intimate parts. With a fellow Scorpio, you can reach a poignant and all-encompassing understanding in the name of emotion, passion, and mutual spiritual maturation. You share a great depth of mind with Pisces—this relationship is decidedly satisfying.

Good pairing

Your natural mistrust can lead to misunderstandings, but stable earth signs make excellent companions: Taurus knows how to break down your negative beliefs, Virgo brings practicality to everyday life, and Capricorn is stoic and determined. Leo and Sagittarius have provocative ways that might pique your ire, but their resourcefulness manages to distract you from your obsessions. Misunderstandings may arise with Cancer due to your stubbornness, but your emotional intelligence will come to the rescue.

Challenging pairing

It's better not to start a relationship with the air signs. They prefer intellectual exploration over emotional intensity and sentimental enthusiasm. They cannot bear the shows of jealousy that you are quick to fall prey to, and their aptitude for freedom and an intense social life contrasts with your search for an all-encompassing and exclusive relationship. You share Aries' tendency for explosive anger—this relationship could include furious arguments.

Magical tips

With the full moon in Scorpio high in the sky, prepare a wine-based infusion to awaken or increase your desire for love. You will need:
- 1 bottle of red wine
- 1 tablespoon grated fresh ginger
- 2 cloves
- Cinnamon flakes
- Orange peel

Pour the wine into a glass—crystal, if possible—add the ginger, cloves, and cinnamon, and leave the infusion to steep for three hours. Pour the mixture through a sieve and into a jug. Pour some wine back into your crystal glass and garnish it with the orange peel. As you sip your love potion, focus your energies on your loved one.

Work

The best

You are an excellent problem-solver, and your determination equals your concentration; when you have a goal in sight, nothing can stop you. If you combine your strengths and skills with another Scorpio, you can complete any project, even the most ambitious, with brilliance and skill. Virgo colleagues are also excellent collaborators—their attention to detail and meticulousness are necessary attributes to help you obtain results that are more than satisfactory. For Capricorn, work is a fundamental area of achievement; your common desire for success unites and exalts you.

Has potential

Yours is the sign least suited for teamwork—sharing is not your strength. Despite their cheerful idealism, Sagittarius can teach you to be flexible when needed. Pisces loves to move from one project to another, while you believe in determination and persistence; despite your differences, they can teach you the fine art of compromise.

To avoid

Few colleagues can sympathize with your dismissive ways and cutting sarcasm. The air signs have an approach to work that is diametrically opposite to yours. They are not very methodical, are often confusing, and tend toward distraction; you will find it impossible to reach an agreement! Fire signs Aries and Leo tend to take credit for every success in their own self-absorbed and conceited ways, unleashing your wrath. Cancer and Taurus have difficulty accepting instructions and making requests.

Magical tips

Tarot is a powerful tool in becoming aware of your desires and can offer interesting suggestions on questions regarding your aspirations.

Try to focus on the goal of your meditation.

1. Draw the card representing your zodiac sign; Scorpio is symbolized by the Card with No Name.
2. Draw the card corresponding to the position of Mars in your birth chart.
3. Draw a card of your choice.

Dwell on the images of the extracted Arcana. What ideas do they evoke in you?

Family

Scorpio parents

Scorpio parents are very protective and gifted with great sensitivity, although their reserve may cause some difficulty in demonstrating their feelings. Energetic and determined and sometimes a little strict, they expect their children to respect the rules established. Despite their impositions, they give their children a large degree of responsibility and are attentive listeners who can pick up on any change of mood in the family.

Scorpio siblings

Scorpio siblings may seem inscrutable, but behind their reserve is a great spirit of observation: they scrutinize every situation to support their brothers and sisters with ready and affectionate advice. They love competition and enjoy challenging their brothers and sisters in exciting and borderline dangerous games. They are a bit possessive—it's better not to steal one of their belongings, as they are inclined to seek revenge.

Family

Magical tips

Use the gemstones connected with your star sign to create beautiful amulets to gift to the people you love: obsidian protects against negative vibrations and eases big changes and the development of intuition; ruby sharpens the mind and gives courage, concentration, optimism, and cheerfulness; jasper facilitates the spirit of initiative and honesty of thought; and fire opal helps people face every new beginning with passion.

Pisces

February 20–
March 20

The last mutable water sign of the zodiac, Pisces is changeable and con-
tradictory: the two fish present in the astrological glyph represent the
duality of those born under this sign. Not surprisingly, the constellation
of Pisces can be seen in the sky between winter and spring. Neptune,
the planet of creativity and spirituality, instills depth of mind as well as interest in the world of the unconscious and spirituality. In the tarot, it is represented by the Hanged Man card, which symbolizes altruism and sacrifice
for the common good but also passive immersion in a contemplative state.

✦ Sun ✦

PERSONALITY AND TEMPERAMENT

You are honest and idealistic, and you don't indulge in sharp judgments. You accept reality and people with kindness, despite your marked tendency toward idealization. Don't let your contradictions scare you.

✦ Moon ✦

EMOTIONS AND EMOTIONAL INTELLIGENCE

The Moon is exalted in your sign, giving you deep feelings and an admirable intuition. Your sensitivity drives you to be empathetic to the pain of others and care for others. You can easily fall prey to illusions.

✦ Ascendant ✦

SOCIABILITY AND SOCIAL LIFE

You are honest and genuine. You would never feign an interest in feeling part of a group or pleasing those around you. You don't like flaunting your sociability and prefer to cultivate your relationships in a reserved way.

✦ Descendant ✦

SUBCONSCIOUS AND DEEP CONNECTIONS

Your Ascendant in Virgo teaches you to seek deep emotional understanding in meeting others and to give yourself with compassion, honesty, and purity.

✦ Mercury ✦

INTELLIGENCE AND COMMUNICATION SKILLS

You have great emotional intelligence and receptivity. You are thoughtful and attentive to detail. Your empathy helps you grasp the nuances of other people's emotions. However, you have some communication difficulties, especially when it comes to making your own needs understood.

✦ Venus ✦

LOVE AND DESIRE

You experience your feelings with sweetness and a little naivety. Venus in Pisces expresses its characteristics to the fullest, giving you the gift of a sublime idea of love that transcends the dualism of the couple and extends in a universal sense. You are looking for unconventional relationships that complete you.

✦ Mars ✦

ACTION AND PASSION

You appear shy and introverted and may seem insecure, but you hide a shrewd and courageous soul when it comes to facing risky situations. You have a tendency to turn your aggression into artistic creation.

Magic
and Pisces

The moon in Pisces is the perfect time for spells to expand consciousness and aid psychic work. The waning moon in Pisces is beneficial for spells that aim to remove negative energy.

Love

Love

Harmonious pairing

Your emotionality urges you to look for a partner who knows how to share a reverie-filled and intense relationship with you. For you, falling in love is a way to live in a dreamy and idealized state of mind. You feel an immediate and overwhelming connection with water signs; sensitive and passionate, you like to spend time together getting lost and indulging in your daydreams.

✦

Good pairing

Despite their tendency toward concreteness, earth signs welcome your seductive, passionate, and imaginative game and can teach you to be more emotionally stable. Sagittarius' callousness may arouse your outrage, but it's one of the few signs that don't wish to dominate you, thanks to their great sense of open-mindedness. Aquarius' fickleness confuses you, but you share common values and a deep sense of justice.

✦

Challenging pairing

Fiery Aries and Leo are too aggressive for you and are definitely not interested in your emotional demands and variegated inner world. Air signs Libra and Gemini are too unstable and extroverted. They wander from one thought to another without any emotional depth, which to you seems superficial and not very satisfying; you will end up unsure about which choices to make, even the most trivial ones.

Magical tips

There is nothing more sacred and powerful than a spiritual bath to access your deepest amorous desires.
You will need:
- 4 pink candles
- 1 glass of milk
- Rose petals

Prepare your bath, placing one candle at each corner. Fill the tub with warm water, then pour in the glass of milk and rose petals; light the candles. Turn off the lights and immerse yourself in the tub, focusing your thoughts on the person you love. When you're ready to get out of the water, collect the petals and place them in a bowl. Keep the bowl next to your bed throughout the night, preferably in the moonlight.

Work

The best

You don't like working under pressure and are intolerant of routine and rules. Thanks to their reserved manner and work ethic, Capricorn is the only colleague who can convince you of the validity of an idea or the feasibility of a project. Pisces colleagues share your values, interests, and approach through emotional understanding. Your communication is clear and linear, and any joint venture will have excellent results.

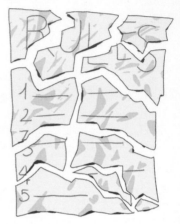

✦

Has potential

You are one of the calmer signs of the zodiac. With their abrupt ways and haste, the fire signs are not in line with your calm approach to work, but their irony can alleviate any work stress. Air signs share your tendency toward distraction; together, you may not be very productive. Taurus might force their point of view, while Scorpio's irreproachable determination might put you off.

✦

To avoid

With their pedantic and meticulous ways, Virgo forces you to be punctual and follow the rules; they are unable to understand that good ideas can also originate from apparently disorganized streams of thought. With Cancer, your problems arise mostly through communication—you often have difficulty sharing your ideas productively and may find yourself bogged down in aimless ramblings.

Magical tips

Tarot is a powerful tool in becoming aware of your desires and can offer interesting suggestions on questions regarding your aspirations.

Try to focus on the goal of your meditation.

1. Draw the card representing your zodiac sign; Pisces is symbolized by the Hanged Man card.
2. Draw the card corresponding to the position of Mars in your birth chart.
3. Draw a card of your choice.

Dwell on the images of the extracted Arcana. What ideas do they evoke in you?

Family

Pisces parents

Pisces parents are excellent at sensing the emotional needs of their family members. They put feelings first and want to base the building of emotional bonds on understanding and emotional sharing in environments full of stimuli. Don't be surprised if they sometimes seem absent; they are unpredictable dreamers and occasionally need to take refuge in their thoughts.

Pisces siblings

Affectionate and empathetic, Pisces would do anything to prevent their siblings from suffering, even taking on responsibilities that are not their own. Their fervent imagination leads them to always invent new games and fantasize about the future. Their ideal playmates are water and air siblings who share their taste for the fantastic.

Magical tips

Use the gemstones connected with your star sign to create beautiful amulets to gift to the people you love: amethyst helps with gaining the right perspective, prevents getting lost in the whirlwind of emotions, drives away guilt, and promotes creativity; amazonite helps to overcome traumas and instills security; and aquamarine represents spiritual wisdom, strengthens intuition, protects against negative vibrations, promotes concentration, and improves attention.

Notes

Notes

Notes

Notes

Ambrosia Hawthorn

Ambrosia Hawthorn is a witch, the founder of *Witchology Magazine*, and the author of *The Spell Book for New Witches*, *Seasons of Wicca*, *The Wiccan Book of Shadows*, and *Anyone Can Be a (Perfect) Witch*. She is a tarot reader, astrologer, and herbalist. Ambrosia's practice is eclectic, and she focuses her craft on the connection between the natural world and inner power. Ambrosia also hosts witchcraft classes at Venefica Cottage.

Silvia Vanni

Italian illustrator Silvia Vanni was born in Castelnuovo di Garfagnana in 1989. A lover of design from a young age, she studied comics and digital coloring at the International School of Comics in Florence. She has published several graphic novels and works as a freelance illustrator. Her passions include tea, Japan, and snow.